All you need to create a world is some crayons. Hare and Bear have a whole box of colored crayons and lots of ideas. In this book they show you how to draw a dinosaur. If you watch how Hare and Bear do it, you can draw one too. Just copy the shapes from the colored box at the top of each page onto your own drawing. And soon you'll be riding through a prehistoric swamp.

Hare and Bear
Draw A Dinosaur
Diann Timms

Reader's Digest Kids
Pleasantville, N.Y.–Montreal

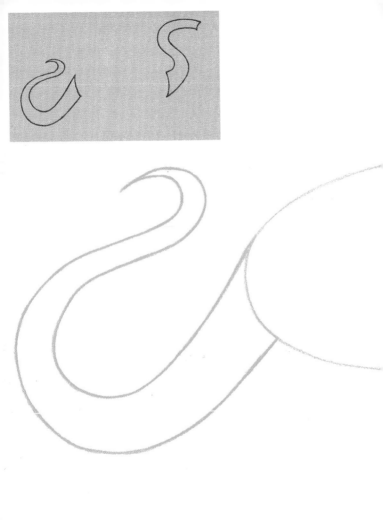

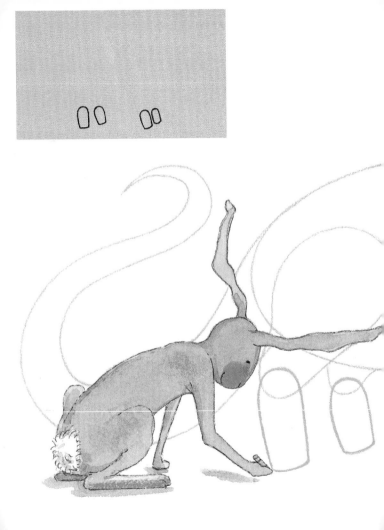

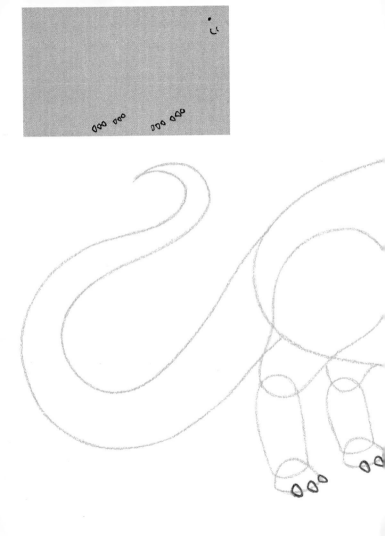

What shall we draw next?

A Reader's Digest Kids Book
Conceived by Diann Timms and Delian Bower Publishing
Copyright © 1993 Diann Timms
All rights reserved. Unauthorized reproduction, in any manner, is prohibited.
Library of Congress Cataloging in Publication data applied for.

ISBN 0–89577–533–6 (v. 3)

ISBN 0–89577–548–4 (set)

Reader's Digest, the Pegasus logo, and Reader's Digest Kids and design
are registered trademarks of The Reader's Digest Association, Inc.

Printed in the United States of America

99 98 97 96 95 94   10 9 8 7 6 5 4 3 2 1

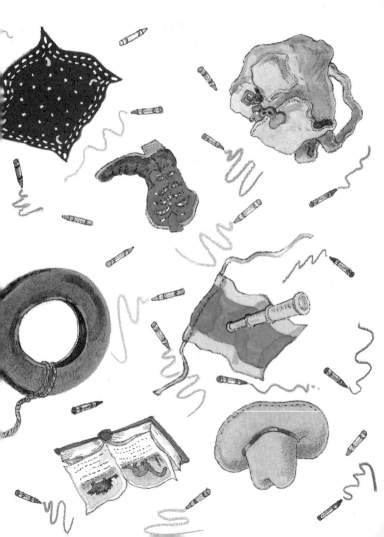